Oddballs, Screwballs & Other Eccentrics

Oddballs, Screwballs & Other Eccentrics

WRITTEN BY FELIX CHEONG
ILLUSTRATED BY CHERYL CHARLI TAN

Marshall Cavendish
Editions

Text © Felix Cheong, Illustrations © Cheryl Tan
© 2020 Marshall Cavendish International (Asia) Private Limited

Published in 2020 by Marshall Cavendish Editions
An imprint of Marshall Cavendish International

A member of the
Times Publishing Group

Other Marshall Cavendish Offices:
Marshall Cavendish Corporation, 800 Westchester Ave, Suite N-641, Rye Brook, NY 10573, USA • Marshall Cavendish International (Thailand) Co Ltd, 253 Asoke, 16th Floor, Sukhumvit 21 Road, Klongtoey Nua, Wattana, Bangkok 10110, Thailand • Marshall Cavendish (Malaysia) Sdn Bhd, Times Subang, Lot 46, Subang Hi-Tech Industrial Park, Batu Tiga, 40000 Shah Alam, Selangor Darul Ehsan, Malaysia

Marshall Cavendish is a registered trademark of Times Publishing Limited

National Library Board, Singapore Cataloguing-in-Publication Data

Name(s): Cheong, Felix. | Tan, Cheryl Charli, illustrator.
Title: Oddballs, screwballs & other eccentrics / written by Felix Cheong ; illustrated by Cheryl Charli Tan.
Description: Singapore : Marshall Cavendish Editions, 2020.
Identifier(s): OCN 1183726683 | ISBN 978-981-4893-27-5 (paperback)
Subject(s): LCSH: Singaporean poetry (English)
Classification: DDC S821--dc23

Printed in Singapore

For Dad and Mom, in remembrance and love.
— Felix

For Jan, and to my family, Ahma and Aunty Lis.
— Cheryl

Contents

Foreword • 11

Baby Questions • 17

Captain Hook's Childhood Dream • 19

Darwin the Champion Sperm Cell • 21

Sticks and Stones • 23

Incommunicado • 25

The Fairy • 27

Rest in Peace, Ma • 29

Parental Pressure • 31

I Have Mom and I Have Mum • 33

Homecoming • 34

Pet Therapy • 37

Peace at Home • 38

The Boy With Webbed Feet • 40

Separation Anxiety • 43

Not Goodbye Yet • 45

The Self-Harming Ghost • 47

The Importance of Hair Grooming • 49

Instructions from St Peter at the Pearly Gates • 51

Otto the Stand-Up Comedian • 53

Hare-Brained • 55

See No Evil • 57

Woes of a Voodoo Doll • 59

The Other • 61

The CatSnake by the Lake • 62

Pass It On • 65

The See-Through Girl • 67

The World's First Female Grim Reaper • 69

Auditioning in the Afterlife • 71

The Ferryman is Lost • 73

Angel Gabriel Grants an Exclusive Interview • 75

The 2021 Calendar Photoshoot Inspired
by the Classics • 77

A Head of the Curve • 79

The Pale Man's Nightmare • 81

Smile and the World Smiles With You • 83

Looking Out for the Elite • 85

Waiting for the Other Shoe to Drop • 87

OK Boomer • 89

Walk This Way • 91

Clock Watcher • 93

The Death of the Forex Trader • 94

The Death of the Weapons Master • 96

What Goes Around • 99

Medusa's Selfie • 101

Rapunzel Sizes Up Her Life • 103

Claire the Astronaut's #ootd • 105

The Cinderella Love Story • 107

Blind Date • 109

The Second Temptation • 111

The Second Temptation II • 113

And the Two Shall Become One • 115

About the Writer • 117

About the Illustrator • 119

Foreword

This is paradoxically the easiest and hardest book I've written.

It came about by accident last year when I chanced upon Cheryl's artwork she had uploaded on Facebook. (Although we were Facebook friends, we didn't know each other formally.) Child-like but threatening, macabre but mischievous, they depict characters crying out for their stories – and back stories – to be explored and told.

To say that I took to these sketches is an understatement. It was more like they had hacked into a past I thought I had double-locked long ago.

I was suddenly 14, the quiet observer always apart from my class; I was the "Beatles freak", as my classmates nicknamed me, who thought it funny to sign myself off as John Lennon.

I was again 17, so socially inept in junior college I terrorised girls by being too upfront with my emotions. And I was 22 once more, floppy-haired and still misplaced in the university, dressed like a New-Wave wannabe with an equally clueless sense of fashion.

In many ways, these poems, taking a through-line in my reading of Edward Lear, Lewis Carroll, Roald Dahl, Tim Burton and Edward Gorey, are very much me as an oddball, screwball and eccentric.

The writing of this book also bookended my parents' death, both from pneumonia, three weeks apart – Dad in December, Mom in January.

It was a difficult time, after the grief and guilt that I had not taken enough care of them over the years, to pick up the pieces. But continue the pen did, and it found strange ways to ink my mourning. Several poems that reimagine the afterlife, such as "Auditioning in the Afterlife", "Instructions from St Peter at the Pearly Gates" and "The Self-Harming Ghost", came from this period.

Oddballs, Screwballs and Other Eccentrics is nothing like what I've written before. And I hope it'll be an experience with poetry you've never had before.

— Felix

"This house has many hearts."

— Poltergeist (1982)

I would like to say that these aren't exactly 'happy' characters. These weird drawings are born of a certain loneliness and sense of entrapment that I did not and still do not know how to deal with. I started drawing these characters during a rather confusing and painful part of my life that I am still stumbling through. I suppose in the middle of the chaos, I simply needed to do something – anything – to bring to life these little imaginary friends that were circling in my head.

Like every other normal kid, I spent great deal of my childhood happily raised on horror films. I'd spend endless weekends with my aunt and my grandparents watching *The*

Exorcist, The Exorcism of Emily Rose, The Omen, The Ring, and *Storm of the Century.* I was an 11-year-old who walked around seeing that old man from *The Poltergeist 2* on overhead bridges, who'd walk into rooms and "sense" things, who'd sit playing with my imaginary friend (Rebecca) whom I never really told anyone about until now (Hi, Rebecca).

Fairytales taught me dreams come true. These stories were all well and important, but horror films taught me about darkness. That sometimes the monsters under our beds and within ourselves have their own stories to tell — stories that need not be confronting, but are worth listening to.

Although it is easy to imagine that the collection of freaks in this book were plucked out of a fictional universe, Felix and I had decidedly set out pretty early on to not romanticise their lives or give them conventional 'happily ever afters'. We wanted to tell stories we felt were relatively absent in our local literary canon — stories that weren't told enough that desperately needed to be told. So while some of these poems are considerably dark, I hope you find some truth or semblance of comfort in them. I hope that our imperfect creatures housed within the pages of this collection will hopefully make you feel less alone in your own darkness too.

So come on into our house. It may be dark, but do not be afraid.

They're here.

— Cheryl

If you've ever had that feeling of loneliness,
of being an outsider, it never quite leaves you.
You can be happy or successful or whatever,
but that thing still stays within you.

— Tim Burton

Baby Questions

"Dada, what are my horns for?"
Carve your name on classroom walls.
Pick the lock of boyfriends' doors.
Gore your way through crowded stores.

"Dada, why do I have wings?"
Flap a breeze when heatwave clings.
Save on fare for flights in spring.
Slap the mouth that makes a din.

"Dada, why is my tail long?'
Reach for things that don't belong.
Tie up bags till airtight strong.
Whip the ass who did you wrong.

Captain Hook's Childhood Dream

I've wanted to be a pirate since young.

It beats being humdrum.

I want to work the decks, skin sun-stung,

Read the wind, beat the drum,

Learn the songs, down the rum.

By hook or by crook, I'll make Mum

See my life belongs to the sea and sun.

I will not accept any crumbs

But captain my own ship, in time to come.

Look, I even have the eyepatch and stump!

Darwin the Champion Sperm Cell

If you want it badly enough,

Find it in yourself to be tough.

Shut out the goody two-shoe fluff.

Work your body, do the hard stuff.

Tune your voice low and make it gruff.

See yourself coming through the rough.

Ignore those who say you are daft.

Do this and you'll have the last laugh

When you are the first to make love

To that cute egg in the buff.

Sticks and Stones

Mommy thought it funny to name me Eve
Since before Christmas Day I was conceived.
She was still laughing when she heaved,
Pushed me out so hard she almost cleaved
And didn't notice the afterbirth serpent leave.

Incommunicado

When your lips have been sewn from young,

Through a pen you hear your own tongue.

Your words have become lines unsung

And held up to the light and hung.

It's a mixed blessing that has sprung

A writer who gives silence lungs.

The Fairy

I wear this costume light as air.

I can be anyone, anywhere,

Flaunt it as my due and my dare.

Free as I am but fully aware

Why I cannot ever declare

Who I am because I am scared

Of Papa who ties me to a nightly chair

And whips manhood into my body bare.

CHERYL

Rest in Peace, Ma

I told you for your wake, I'd wear my Sunday best –
Your apron and your long black dress –
And for once, I have a prayer clasped to my chest.
So you can give your big mouth a much-needed rest.
My life may yet be one big mess
But I'm sure as hell done with one of your tests.

Parental Pressure

Chuck wasn't sure why his folks were fighting over him.
From morning they quarrelled till the sun dimmed,
Round and around the same issue they skimmed.

"Chuck should learn the piano," Mom said. "It's meant to be."
Dad said, "Playing rock guitar is what brings in money."
Before long, pots and fists were thrown indiscriminately.

Down the middle his family did split.
Chuck ended up living with Mom but still felt adrift.
No one asked him what he wanted of his Gift.

That day, after he had had his biggest dump,
He removed the keyboard attached to his stump
And instantly felt so light he could hum.

Chuck got his hand into saws and screws
And set about making his own stool.
And that was how he chased away the blues.

I Have Mom and I Have Mum

Sometimes Mum pampers me.

But I keep mum

Because Mom doesn't want Mum to treat me differently.

Sometimes Mom canes me.

But I keep mum

Because Mom doesn't want me to be treated differently.

Sometimes friends tease me.

But I keep mum

Because I don't want Mom to know I am treated differently.

Sometimes Mom fights with Mum

Because Mum keeps mum

When people treat us differently.

I have Mom and I have Mum.

But I don't keep mum

Because I don't want us to be treated differently.

Homecoming

All his life, Quid never felt he belonged.
He could swim as well as his siblings could.
But something about his free style was wrong.
They laughed he was as graceful as driftwood.

And Quid could not look more different from them.

Long and awkward was the shape of his head.

He thought it looked quite like a piece of gem.

They quipped it was more like condom instead.

Quid asked his dad why he was born different.

"Mom has a fetish for eating plastic."

His mom was equally irrelevant.

"I must've taken too much antibiotics."

It was obvious to one and all with eyes

That Quid must've come with adoption papers.

It would explain why when live octopi

Became the 'in' thing for human dinner,

Quid was quickly thrown out with the garbage.

Watching his family being consumed alive,

He felt neither attachment nor outrage

But so much relief he took a deep dive.

There, he came across others just like him,

With their alien heads and their zigzag ways.

They passed out ink and they turned his home dim.

That was how Quid spent the rest of his days.

Pet Therapy

You learn the essence of being

In the crow you take under your wing.

You may not dress to the nines or sing.

You may never find a boy worth keeping

Or keep your family from self-destructing.

But this you know when the world is failing,

Your crow will give your scars a sound hearing.

Peace at Home

You return to your blue flat
And you smell a blue rat
Sitting on the blue mat.

You hear your blue cat
Yelling inside the blue rat
That it lost the combat.

Before you go tit for tat
With a very long blue bat,
You strategise that

Killing the blue rat
Is killing your blue cat.
No two ways around that.

You give it a pat
And sit down for a chat
With the blue rat on the mat.

With skills of a diplomat,
You soon arrive at
A treaty from the spat.

The blue rat will not scat
Or digest your blue cat
When there's food on the blue mat.

So you now have two pets
To feed in your blue flat.
And there is peace after that.

The Boy With Webbed Feet

There was some dispute between Pete and Buck
If they should name the new boy Frog or Duck.

He had webbed feet and walked with a waddle
That was easy to mimic and trip over.

But he would croak like a frog when he fell,
Especially when they threw him in the well.

Before long, they came to a consensus
To call him Fruck for all game purposes.

It was fun to pun on their cleverness!
From "Frucker" to "motherfrucking highness",

They swore within reasonable limits,
Out of earshot of their teacher-dimwits.

When Fruck didn't climb out of the well one night,
The two boys panicked and quickly took flight.

Pete tripped over a rock and cracked his head,
Spilled its contents over his family's gate.

Buck fell into a manhole and he yelped.
No one heard his last word on earth was "help".

The police soon found the Boy with Webbed Feet,
Having his fun in water ten feet deep.

"Thanks to Pete and Buck, I've learned how to swim!
And I know what I can do with these limbs."

Separation Anxiety

Katie could not understand why
She and Craig had to separate.
She could see him drawing away
As slow as night from dawn in the sky.
Frantically she waved but time didn't wait
For her linger to have its say.

Dad said, "It is time for goodbye."
Mom said, "It is for the best, Kate."
Granny said, "You'll meet again someday."
No one took the time to explain why.
No one gave her an answer straight
And no one could make him stay.

Years later, when Kate recalled his eyes,
How they were sad and full of weight,
She knew, and snuffed her flame in the ashtray.

Not Goodbye Yet

Death called out my name,
And it always sounded the same.
"Don't you want my fame?
That's the nature of the game.
Jump. There is no shame."
As close to the edge I came,
But I got it tamed
Till tomorrow, again.

The Self-Harming Ghost

You can't find knives
In the afterlife.

No one has pens
They're willing to lend.

There's nothing sharp
On which you can harp.

As much as you need,
No matter how deep

You cut your arms,
You can't come to harm.

Only these scars
Remind you how far

You hurt yourself
Before your farewell.

The Importance of Hair Grooming

"A trim moustache gives you gravitas,"
The demon confessed without being asked.
"It makes you appear wise and just.
You agree it's a professional must?"

He did look like he was up to the task –
Confident, genial and not in a rush.
"Find me a barber I can trust,"
I said and died without a fuss.
There was little else to discuss
But let his claws carry my spirit fast
To that hair salon among stardust.

Instructions from St Peter at the Pearly Gates

Three keys you have to account for:
One to open the main door,
One just to open the floor,
The last for the corridor.

Opening the floor before
The door and the corridor,
You see right to the earth's core
And a drop to hell in store.

Opening the corridor
Before the floor and the door,
Infinite dark comes to the fore
And you're in it evermore.

The trick is open the door,
The corridor, then the floor.
Not the door and then the floor,
Followed by the corridor.

Do it this way, that's the law,
And you'll get key number four.
Where it leads no one foresaw.
Not even I been there before.

Otto the Stand-Up Comedian

I may have two arms short of eight,
But they bear more than my weight
So I escape being somebody's bait.

I may have an eye short of two,
But I'm more focused in what I do,
And I escaped serving the army too.

I may not have all God's blessings –
Maybe I came late for his fitting –
But I escaped his wrath and beatings.

If I turn my half-cup upside down
And tip the bar for one more round,
My life is perfect, pound for pound.

For how else can I be up on stage
Without those years of bottled rage
Or rattling misery's tender cage?

Hare-Brained

For the sake of science, I agreed
To the experimental surgery.
I had lost my head, to a degree,
Sentenced to the death penalty
For killing a widow for her money.
But the face that gazed back at me
Was this weird Donnie Darko bunny.

"It'll grow on you," the doc said helpfully.
"Rabbits are not prone to violent tendency."
True enough, I've since been so crime-free
I must thank the state for its carrot of mercy.

See No Evil

Three blind boys who saw no evil
Met up to look for the Devil
On a dark night most medieval.
"We will keep it civil
And ask why he sought upheavals
When love is what keeps us stable."
Despite their good faith in keeping things level,
No one came but fans of heavy metal
Celebrating one hell of a rock festival.

Woes of a Voodoo Doll

You think I like living with pins
And needles? Every curse is akin
To slow death by pricks of skin,
From head to southmost-end of shin.
A grim job no one takes on the chin
But I do it with a shrug and grin,
Dulled by generous pints of gin.
I can't even tell my next-of-kin
All your evil thoughts I hold within.

The Other

After years of being wound,
I've finally come round
I won't be pinned down
To anything sound.
My features aren't found
Anywhere in town.
To you, I am bound
To be some kind of clown.
But hold that thought now
As I let you drown
I've become your monster
From deep underground.

The CatSnake by the Lake

I saw a cat by the lake
That looked almost like a snake.

I must've done a double take
And confirmed it wasn't a fake.

There was a lot here at stake –
I pinched myself hard awake.

"Are you some kind of outbreak,
A disease of cat and snake?"

He smiled at the way I quaked.
"Sir, you can call me CatSnake.

Dad was a cool cat named Jake,
Mom a quick snake surnamed Blake."

"But what are you, for God's sake?
Neither head nor tail I make!"

He laughed as he chewed his steak.
"What you said must take the cake!

Look at yourself, so half-baked –
Your fish tail and lion head.

Don't forget and don't forsake.
It's your past you cannot shake."

Ashamed of what I had raked,
I dove tail-first in the lake.

Pass It On

It was the hymn that changed his life.
"It only takes a spark
To get a fire going."

That was it; one sentence so rife
With meaning, it made its mark
And got Anson going.

Sometimes, he would involve his wife
Who loved to set alight parks
Before she got going.

Often, he was alone, a drive
To somewhere on a lark
And he got it going.

There was never any doubt or strife.
Fire was his calling; it burned the dark
And got him going. And going.

The See-Through Girl

⚜

I'm paid well to be a nude model
Since artists love sketching my bones and muscles.
I'm paid well to sprawl on the table
For doctors to probe me with their scalpel.

Just from not eating many weeks over,
I've become this thing of instant wonder.
I finally look good enough for the camera
Though my heart is slowly going under.

⚜

The World's First Female Grim Reaper

It takes a woman to do a man's job.

I know, because everyone else is a flop.

Bill is too weak and so is Bob.

Nick can't bring himself to kill heartthrobs

And I have to save him from fan mobs.

As for Tom, he ends up in sobs

And I get him in time out of the tight spot.

So never send two-bit slobs

To scythe lives you want to rob.

Auditioning in the Afterlife

"What do you mean there is no role
For me? Ask my agent, bless her soul.
Before I'm even cold in the hole,
Fanny wakes me up. 'Hey, roll
Over. Put your eternal rest on hold.
They're making a movie down below.
A remake of *Corpse Bride*, I'm told.
Good chance for you to get into the fold.
So, chop, chop. Dress up. Put on some kohl.'

Here I am, ready to roll.
It's a mob film? I can go with the flow.
What's it called? *Cops Bribe*. Oh.
I'm overdressed then. Lol."

The Ferryman is Lost

Mother Fish was woken up by an oar,
Stirring yawning waves on the River Styx.
She had not seen this Ferryman before.
Obviously, he had not learned the trade tricks.

"Where are you heading this misty evening?"
The Ferryman shrugged. "I'm new around here.
I'm rowing but round the same spot I'm circling.
I'm due to pick up a dead passenger."

"Smell it?" Father Fish said, taking a breath.
Why couldn't Hades give these young people training?
"Just follow the terrible stench of death.
You will know it when your nose starts flaring."

The Ferryman sniffled. "I have a cold,
So I won't get far if I use my nose.
I've to hurry to earn my coins of gold.
Don't you have GPS or something close?"

Angel Gabriel Grants an Exclusive Interview

You mean you did not know these wings
Are for show and don't do a thing?

You may touch them – so soft, right?
Creation's finest quill, so light.

Travelling without flight is a skill.
If I tell you, I have to kill...

Never mind. Secrets of the trade!
I bring the news and I get paid.

The medium and message must fit.
No right or wrong way about it.

I try to make it mystical,
Like a Hollywood spectacle,

So people wouldn't see me and scream
Or wave me off as a bad dream.

You could say that – let's not be coy.
I'm a singing telegram boy.

The 2021 Calendar Photoshoot Inspired by the Classics

Why am I here?

I don't even like Shakespeare.

Well, maybe some parts of *King Lear*.

This feels decidedly queer.

Whose skull is it? Oh dear.

I think I need a few beers

To hide my shaky veneer.

Maybe I should quit, for I fear

I will disappoint my peers

As the only disabled who can't fill

This tokenism of the year.

A Head of the Curve

They told me to study hard, get a head.
So I followed their ambition and said
All the right things and made
Sure I got it screwed down straight.
But the head I had chosen never quite paid
Off. Nothing was as easy as it was laid
Out, so I ended up being detached instead.

The Pale Man's Nightmare

I dreamt I had eyes in the right place
On a smooth template of face.
I could be mistaken for any race.
I did not need to keep my tongue laced.
I was average and fully erased,
A high-functioning nutcase.
In cold sweat, I woke up, displaced,
Thanked God I was myself and not effaced.

Smile and the World Smiles With You

They called him the Smiley Chameleon.
He had a smile fit for any occasion.
On happy days, it would spell contentment
But on bad days, sheer disillusionment.
It could beam patriotism for the nation,
Or sympathy for bereavement.
It was as sweet as any politician's,
Or devious by its own admission.

He had a smile so exact in calibration,
Yet natural in its deliberation,
You could rent it, wholly or in instalments,
Put it on and become recognisably human.

Looking Out for the Elite

Two eyes good, four eyes better.
We look for people who can see so much further,
So much deeper and so much wider,
So much longer and so much harder,
So much higher and so much quicker,
So much area and so much to cover
So much so we do not consider
Who else but people like us matter.

Waiting for the Other Shoe to Drop

Isn't life about hanging around
Till you are two feet underground?

You are happy one day, then sad;
You do it right, then things go bad.

You toe the line every day in school.
But that's not what the cool kids do.

You fall head over heels with her.
But it's your father she prefers.

You wear your soul out in your job.
But the promotion strolls to Rob.

Everywhere you turn, you're stepped on.
Your sole meaning in life is gone.

All you can do is dig your heels in.
Try your best not to move an inch.

OK Boomer

⚜

One day, when you're aged and weak,

You can't get by without a stick,

Not to keep you from a fatal trip,

But to beat conformity out of the meek.

⚜

Walk This Way

Walk this way
Every day.
I feel fine
Past my prime.
I'm stiffer,
I shuffle.
I tremble,
I wobble.
No hurry.
No worry.
I still walk,
It's my talk.
I lost wife
Rest of life.
If I fall,
Death takes all.
It's my turn,
No return.

Clock Watcher

No matter how many hours a day spans,
Twenty-seven or thirty-six,
You will never live long enough to fix
All the problems on your hands.

The Death of the Forex Trader

Something was amiss when he woke up at noon.
He found he had three malignant balloons.

"I can't afford to look this unpleasant.
Bad things only happen to plebeian peasants."

Of course, he was not vain, not by a bit.
Still, he draped a bespoke scarf over it.

All day, a hiss went through his whole body,
Like flash surges of electricity.

He could scream but he exercised control,
For he did not want the whole world to know.

He kept his head and his friends in the dark.
"Illness shall not blight my name in their heart."

As he was about to leave his office,
Bloody hell broke loose from his orifice.

The press next day went into great detail
Of the forex trader's splattered entrails.

A crew of twenty took months to clean up
His body parts and every spot of blood.

By then, markets had crashed and all was blown.
There was barely enough for his tombstone:

"Money gives you pride, money gives you face.
But don't count on money to die with grace."

The Death of the Weapons Master

Q was a weapons master beyond rebuke.
But he was told the Queen would've made him Duke
If he had been the first one to build the nuke.

"Not your fault the US did it years ago,"
She said when his royal knighthood was bestowed.
But Q still felt a big thrust through his ego.

He spent the next six years in the laboratory,
Never once visiting the lavatory.
Meals and baths were also not mandatory.

Q let his imagination run loose
And built gadgets the MI6 spies could use.
Like a plague diffuser hidden in a goose,

A tie that snapped your neck off with a quick swish,
A blowpipe for you to aim a pufferfish
And jelly that turned your insides into warm squish.

He'd never kept up with the bodies done in.
Science had no conscience, not to Q's reckoning.
To think otherwise would've led to his ruin.

"We keep count only of our own death," Q said
When shot by his own boomerang arrowhead
Fired an hour earlier and pumped full of lead.

He must've forgotten how it would come round,
Without any remorse and without a sound,
To find its target at the very same ground.

Q left the world exactly as he found it –
A queue of weapons masters who saw it fit
To assume his job and create the next hit.

What Goes Around

Life was as well as dull could be.

I wasn't sure, for the life of me,

Why I ate a live octopus readily.

It came to me so naturally

I downed ten more, despite my allergy.

And when the tentacles came, so did TV

And, of course, the seafood endorsement money.

For a spell, things went swimmingly.

But now, life is as dull as well can be.

I still can't grasp the situation fully.

Medusa's Selfie

Would you like me more if I pose silly,
Like *The Scream* being posed by Macaulay?
Could you see me as I am, not an ugly
With a head that hisses but a homebody
With untamed hair that just needs a trim monthly?
Aren't you dying to see the beauty
Frozen like a princess inside this selfie?

Rapunzel Sizes Up Her Life

What good is hair that's Instagrammable
When I can't score a goddamn commercial
Or appear on bloody *Singapore Social*?

I know I don't amass the same numbers
As these impossibly perfect influencers
With their millions of ant-like followers.

It doesn't help I'm locked in this tower.
The backdrop is staid, the angles are fewer,
The wifi sucks and my posts aren't quicker.

I might have to do nudes to up my game.
Tease but not reveal too much in the frame.
And yes, it's time to change my stupid name.

Sounds like a brand of cheap conditioner.
"Rinse your hair well with Rapunzel
And you'll keep it long and glowing forever."

Claire the Astronaut's #ootd

Claire wasn't sure what she should wear.
Being the first was a nightmare –
Always in the camera's glare –
And she'd need to flaunt her flair,
An outfit to match her hair.
So many things to take care!

Her body was cold but fair
In a dress like solar flare
When they found it high up there.
Without her helmet and air,
She still had beauty to spare.
Death had styled her beyond repair.

The Cinderella Love Story

I've had dates who thought they'd succeed

Talking about planting their seed.

I've met studs and duds, a few steeds,

Even an Afro-Chinese Swede

Who looked like he could do with some speed.

None could stand up to the Centipede.

He wasn't your garden-variety breed.

He had old money but not its greed,

Not too flashy, none too twee.

So when he showed off all his title deeds,

I said "yes!" so fast I got a nosebleed.

Blind Date

"So, you were born in the year of the goat?"

It was the first question she'd always float,

Just to make sure they were in the same boat.

It wouldn't do to lose time she'd devote

To sex and find out he was one Zodiac sign remote.

"Of course," he said without meaning to gloat.

"I even have the prerequisite looks!"

She was his first try at sowing wild oats.

But also his last. For he barely croaked

When she clinically slit his mutton throat.

The Second Temptation

"So, do you see," said the serpent
Trying not to turn it into a sermon,
"Eve's greed had led to your eviction
From a paradise of enjoyment.
Don't you think it's time to get even?"

Adam slept on it but was certain
Revenge was out of the question.
For who else but Eve would cook the bacon,
Keep house and his stock of beer current,
Wash his car and mind the children?
Her life had virtually become her prison –
There was no need for other punishment.

The Second Temptation II

Weeks after she had left her husband,
Eve came across again the serpent.
He still lisped but had had speech lessons.
"I see you have a bun in the oven.
Knowing Adam, he might be reluctant
To add one more mouth to your six children.
Why don't you feed your unborn to the ravens?"

Eve sat still for several moments,
Then got up all of a sudden.
"Enough of your tales and stupid reasons!"
She knotted his forked tongue into a tight ribbon,
Threw him back into the Garden
And walked into her sunset a free person.

And the Two Shall Become One

⚜

When they gave me your beloved eye,

It opened the vastness of my sky,

But I didn't see you for last goodbyes.

After they grafted your gentle claws,

I felt your knowing caress once more

Before they took you down the hall.

You are now in me as I in you.

No lovers possess a love so true.

This body we share. We do, I do.

⚜

About the Writer

Felix Cheong is the author of 17 books, including five volumes of poetry, a trilogy of satirical flash fiction and three children's picture books. His works have been widely anthologised and nominated for the prestigious Frank O'Connor Award and the Singapore Literature Prize. Conferred the Young Artist Award in 2000 by the National Arts Council, he holds a master's in creative writing and is currently an adjunct lecturer with the National University of Singapore, Murdoch University, University of Newcastle and Curtin University.

About the Illustrator

Cheryl Charli Tan never saw herself as an illustrator and has, until recently, has only done art as a hobby. She is an aspiring circus artist and theatre practitioner passionate about experimental works incorporating film, installation, sound, movement and visual art. She writes for Bandwagon Asia, Popspoken.sg and Plural Art Mag. When she is not geeking out over the latest horror film, superhero, or sci-fi flick, Cheryl buries herself in circus arts, music, film, art, photography, and sociology — amongst other things like astronomy, dinosaurs, literature, comic books and cats.